Snakes

By Sally Cowan

Snakes have no legs.
They bend from side to side
to slide on stones
and sand dunes.

Snakes have long spines with lots of bones.

A snake has lots of scales on its skin.

A snake's skin can have spots and lines.

This snake uses its spots and lines to hide.

Can you see the snake?

A snake's home is in a den.

A den can be in a hole.

It can be in a cave, too.

When the sun shines,
snakes like to doze
on a hot rock.

Some snakes are safe.

Snakes do not like us,
so they hide from us.

Some snakes have
two fangs.

Those snakes can bite!

Do not get close to them!

CHECKING FOR MEANING

1. What do snakes use to hide? *(Literal)*
2. Where do snakes live? *(Literal)*
3. Why might snakes not like people? *(Inferential)*

EXTENDING VOCABULARY

spines	What is a snake's spine like? Where is your spine? What other animals have spines?
scales	What does the word *scales* mean in the text? What other creatures have scales? Can you think of another meaning for the word *scales*?
fangs	What part of a snake is a fang? What is the difference between a fang and a tooth?

MOVING BEYOND THE TEXT

1. What other animals can you think of that have no legs? How do they move?
2. Snakes use the patterns on their skin to hide. How do other animals hide?
3. What should you do if you see a snake?
4. Do you feel differently about snakes after reading this book? Why?

TIME TO WRITE

Write about what you can do to stay safe from snakes when you're playing outside.

PRACTICE WORDS

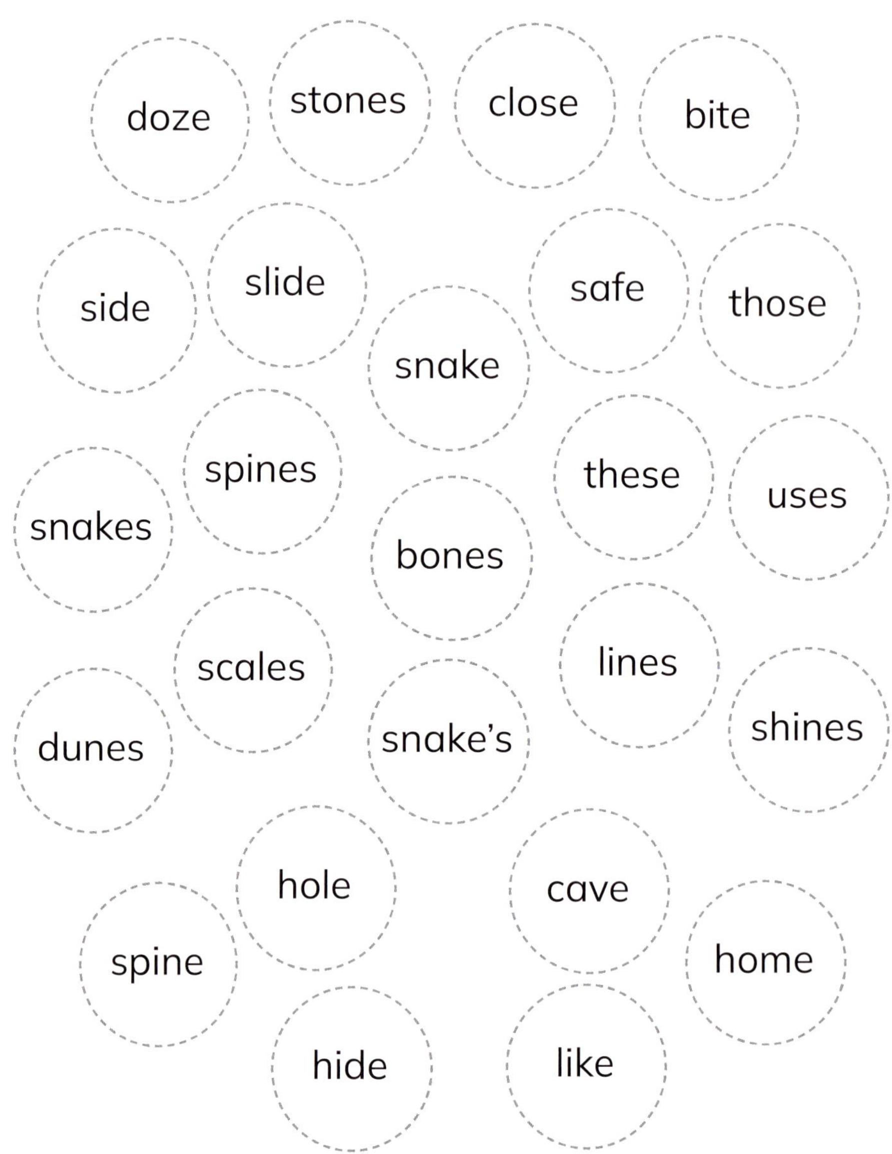